C000152465

BRITAIN SINCE WORLD WAR II

Immigration

COLIN HYNSON

W

FRANKLIN WATTS
LONDON • SYDNEY

First published in 2007 by
Franklin Watts
338 Euston Road
London NW1 3BH

Franklin Watts Australia
Level 17/207 Kent Street
Sydney NSW 2000
Copyright © Franklin Watts 2007

Editor: Jeremy Smith
Art director: Jonathan Hair
Design: Jason Anscomb
Picture researcher: Sophie Hartley

All rights reserved.
A CIP catalogue record for this book
is available from the British Library.

Picture credits: Advertising Archives:
11. Alamy: 18t, 19, 22b, 23t, 24b. Bob
Jones Photography/Alamy: 16. Corbis:
6t, 15t, 13t. Easyjet: 25t. Getty images:
10t, 17, 20, 22t, 24t, 26t. Sally and
Richard Greenhill/Alamy: 24b.
istockphoto: 6b, 7, 9b, 10b, 12, 18b,
21, 25b, Photofusion Picture
Library/Alamy: 15b, 23b,
popperfoto.com. 8 tr. Ben
Ramos/Alamy. 8tl. Time Life
Pictures/Getty Images: 9t. VIEW
Pictures Ltd/Alamy: 8b.

Dewey Classification: 941.2

ISBN: 978 0 7496 7606 3

Printed in China

Franklin Watts is a division of
Hachette Children's Books, an
Hachette Livre UK company.

CONTENTS

From Roman times to the present day, people from all over the world have made Britain their new home. They came to escape war and famine or simply to find a new life for themselves. After the end of the British Empire, this trend became even greater. Each new group of immigrants has helped to create the Britain that we know today.

▲ A map of the British Empire (areas shown in red) at its height in 1875.

THEN AND NOW

It is estimated that in the 18th century the African population in Britain was about 10,000. According to the 2001 census there were about 480,000 people of African descent living in Britain.

THE RISE OF EMPIRE

Between the start of the 17th century and the end of the 19th century, Britain created a huge empire. The islands of the Caribbean were controlled by Britain from the 17th century, while India and large parts of Africa became part of the British Empire in the late 18th and 19th centuries. Many people in these parts of the world saw Britain as their "motherland". After World War II (1939-1945), they responded to a call from the British government for workers to come to Britain.

AFRICANS IN BRITAIN

There have been black and Asian people in Britain for hundreds of years. From the 1570s, African slaves were brought to Britain, and it became fashionable amongst the wealthy to have a black servant. From the 1700s, the number of Africans began to grow. Many of them worked as servants but they also worked in British ports.

▼ The black trumpeter John Blanke was one of a number of black servants in Tudor England.

▲ An illustration showing Irish harvesters on their way to England to find work.

ASIANS IN BRITAIN

The first record of an Asian living in Britain was in 1616, when an Indian called Peter was baptised in London. From the 18th century Asian servants (called ayahs) and sailors (called lascars) were recruited to work in Britain.

OTHER IMMIGRANTS

A famine in Ireland between 1845 and 1850 forced many Irish people to come to this country. From the start of the 19th century many Italians made Britain their home. In the 1860s, there were about 2,000 Italians living in London. Jews from Russia and Eastern Europe settled in Britain from the 1880s. By the end of the century there were over 120,000 Jews living in this country.

❝ *I ... bought some bread and cheese, and coal, and carried it home. My dear wife was rejoiced to see me return with something to eat... The first nobility of the land never made a better meal.* ❞

The memories of Ukawsaw Gronniosaw, an African who lived in England in the 1760s. He was a weaver in Norwich but he often found it difficult to find any kind of work.

BUZZ BOX

People who came to settle in Britain from the same place tended to live close to each other. In the 19th century, Clerkenwell in London had so many Italians living there that it was known as "Little Italy".

TIMELINE

410
Saxons begin to migrate to England.

880
The Vikings arrive in England.

1066
Both the Normans and Jews start to settle in Britain.

1509
The first record of an African in Scotland.

1509
John Blanke employed by Henry VIII as a trumpeter.

1616
The first mention of an Asian living in Britain.

1845–50
The start of large-scale immigration from Ireland to Britain.

1880s
Jews begin to arrive in Britain from Eastern Europe in large numbers.

AFRICAN-CARIBBEAN IMMIGRATION

Many of the islands of the Caribbean had been part of the British Empire since the 17th century. Slaves from Africa worked on the sugar plantations. Later, Caribbean soldiers fought for Britain in both World Wars. They had been taught that Great Britain was their "motherland" and this is one of the reasons why so many decided to come to the UK.

THE EMPIRE WINDRUSH

In 1946, the SS *Empire Windrush* stopped off in Jamaica to pick up some men who were coming to England. They had served in the RAF during World War II and were returning to their units. Many more men decided to travel on the *Windrush* to see if they could find work in Britain. The ship arrived at Tilbury, London, on 22nd June 1948, with 500 people on board. It was the start of Caribbean immigration to Britain.

LOOKING FOR WORK

During the 1950s, there was a shortage of workers in Britain and people from the Caribbean were encouraged to come to Britain. Throughout the 1950s and 1960s Caribbean men and women made sure that British hospitals were looking after the sick and that the buses and trains ran on time.

BUZZ BOX

After 1948, between 500 and 700 Caribbean people arrived in Britain every year. Between 1951 and 1953, this rose to over 2,000 a year. In 1954, 10,000 arrived, and in the next year the number was 27,000. In 1956, over 40,000 Caribbean citizens journeyed to Britain to start a new life.

▲ The ship SS *Empire Windrush* brought the first group of West Indian immigrants to Britain.

> " *My parents brought me on the* **Windrush** *– I had no choice in the matter. They didn't have to – it was obvious they came in search of a better life, better opportunities. I had never been out of Kingston same as for anybody, to go on this big ship, for all those days, it was quite an experience.* "
>
> Vince Reid from Jamaica, one of the passengers on the *Windrush*

◄ Some of the first immigrants from Jamaica study a British paper, looking for work.

▲ Riots break out in Notting Hill, London in the 1950s.

TIMELINE

1914-1918
Caribbean soldiers fight in World War I.

1939-1945
Caribbean men and women help Britain in World War II.

June 22nd 1948
The arrival of the SS *Empire Windrush*.

1962
Jamaica becomes independent.

1966
Barbados becomes independent.

1955-1962
250,0000 people arrive from the Caribbean.

August 1958
Race riots in Nottingham and Notting Hill.

August 1959
First Notting Hill Carnival.

THE NOTTING HILL RIOTS

Like many other immigrants, Caribbean people tended to live together in the same place. They moved to large cities like Liverpool and Manchester but most stayed in London. One of the areas of London that Caribbean people settled in was Notting Hill in west London. In August 1958 there were fights between black and white people in the city of Nottingham. At the end of that month Notting Hill was the scene of a week of violent attacks on Caribbean people, mostly by white "Teddy Boys" (so called because they dressed in Edwardian-style suits). In 1959, the very first Notting Hill Carnival was held by the Caribbean community as a response to the previous year's violence.

CLOSING THE DOOR

The Notting Hill riots started a debate in Britain about immigration and about the need to control the number of people coming to Britain. In 1962, Parliament passed a law called the Commonwealth Immigrants Act. This restricted the number of people from the Commonwealth, including the Caribbean, who could come to this country. Caribbean immigration slowed down to a trickle.

THEN AND NOW

Between 1955 and 1962, about 250,000 people from the Caribbean migrated to Britain. Most stayed and made Britain their new home. By 2001, the African-Caribbean population of Britain had grown to over 560,000 – still less than one per cent of the population of this country.

By the end of the 1960s, Caribbean immigration had more or less stopped. From that time until the present day, people from the Caribbean community have become an important part of British society. However, racism and discrimination have meant that they have had to struggle to take their rightful place in Britain.

▲ Riots in Brixton, London in 1981.

FACING DISCRIMINATION

From the start of the 1970s, Britain went through an economic recession and unemployment rose across the country. Unemployment in the Caribbean community was greater than amongst white people. Many blamed racial discrimination for this. Young Caribbean people also felt that they were being treated unfairly by the police. In 1981, these two grievances led to large-scale rioting in British cities. The first riot started on 11th April, 1981, in Brixton in London. Other cities with large Caribbean populations also saw riots that year. These included Liverpool, Manchester, Birmingham and Bristol.

FIGHTING DISCRIMINATION

As a result of the riots the government asked Lord Scarman to look at the reasons behind the riots. He decided that the Caribbean community needed extra help to fight discrimination and to build trust between the police and Caribbean people. This trust was damaged by the murder of

▶ The award-winning writer Zadie Smith. Her mother is from Jamaica and her father is from England.

The Notting Hill Carnival is the largest carnival in Europe. In 1976 about 150,000 people watched the carnival. Now over one million people go every year to see the floats and listen to the music.

1962
Commonwealth Immigrants Act passed by Parliament.

1976
Fighting at Notting Hill Carnival.

1978
Viv Anderson is the first black footballer to play for England.

1981
Riots in cities throughout Britain.

1984
Tessa Sanderson is the first Caribbean person to win an Olympic gold for Britain.

1985
Riots in cities throughout Britain.

1987
The first Caribbean MPs are elected.

1993
Murder of Stephen Lawrence.

1999
McPherson report published.

> *We are really more of a British thing. I mean, now black Britain has all types of things to be proud of. I think I'm a bit of both really. I'm black and I'm definitely British, and that's what I am.*
>
> **Jazzy B, the founder of Soul II Soul**

◄ A survey carried out in 2004 revealed over 20 per cent of players in the English Premier League were of Caribbean descent, including Rio Ferdinand (left).

Stephen Lawrence in April 1993, when it was believed that the police did little to find his killers. A report by Sir William McPherson showed that the police still treated Caribbean people unfairly.

MAKING PROGRESS

Over the past few decades the Caribbean community has had a huge impact on many aspects of British life. In 1987, the first MPs from the Caribbean community were elected to Parliament. British music owes a lot to Caribbean musicians and DJs like Eddie Grant, Soul II Soul and Goldie. The world of sport has also benefited from Caribbean sportspeople. Linford Christie and Tessa Sanderson became famous athletes. Rio Ferdinand and Aaron Lennon play football for England. British literature has also been enriched by writers and poets such as Zadie Smith and Benjamin Zephaniah.

THEN AND NOW

In 1950 Lloyd Delapenha was the only Caribbean footballer playing for a major English club. In today's game, around 13 per cent of all professional footballers are now of Caribbean descent.

ASIAN IMMIGRATION

There have been people from the Indian sub-continent living in Britain since the 17th century. In the 19th century, many Asians came to work as servants, nannies or sailors. It was in the 1950s that large scale immigration from Asian countries really started, and it continued until the 1970s.

▼ An Asian mother and her three children arrive at a British airport from India during the 1960s.

THE NEED FOR WORKERS

There were two reasons why Asian immigration began in the 1950s. The first was that India and Pakistan became independent from Britain in 1947. There was conflict between the two countries around the border areas of Punjab and Gujarat. This encouraged many Indian and Pakistani people to look to Britain as a safe place to start a new life. At the same time there was a shortage of workers in Britain, and Indians and Pakistanis were encouraged to come and work here.

DIFFERENT INDUSTRIES

Pakistanis from the Punjab region were the first group to arrive in Britain in the middle of the 1950s. They were needed to work in the textile industries that were based in the north of England. Towns such as Rochdale and

What's your name?

▲ Children from India and Pakistan receive English lessons at a school in Walsall, 1958.

❝*The bulky serving counters were replaced with rows of modern self-service shelves packed with masalas and daals as well as baked beans and cornflakes. The outside bulged with exotic fresh vegetables and fruit like mangoes, doodhi and karela.*❞

Anoo Gupta talking about Asian shops in Manchester in the 1960s

THEN AND NOW

In 1966 there were about 360,000 people in Britain who were of Indian or Pakistani origin (about 0.8 per cent of Britain's population). In 2001, that figure was over two million (about four per cent of Britain's population).

Bradford soon had a growing Asian population. A few years later, Indians and Pakistanis arrived in London and the Midlands. They worked in factories and for the National Health Service (NHS).

FAMILY BUSINESSES

At first it was mostly single men that came to live in Britain. During the 1960s, family members came to join them. With the whole family in Britain, many Asian people began to start their own businesses. These included grocery stores, clothing shops and restaurants. These businesses first served just the Asian community but they soon started to sell things to the wider population.

▼ Since the 1960s Asians have opened up many businesses, from grocery stores to restaurants.

BUZZ BOX

Many Sikhs came to Britain from the Punjabi area of India. Like the other Asian communities they tended to settle in the same area of Britain. Many Sikhs moved to Southall in London.

TIMELINE

1947
India and Pakistan become independent from Britain and war breaks out between the two countries.

1950s
Asian workers begin to arrive in Britain.

1952
First free elections in India.

1958
The army takes over the government of Pakistan.

1962
First Commonwealth Immigration Act (see page 9).

1965
War between India and Pakistan.

1968
Second Commonwealth Immigration Act distinguishes UK passport holders who had the right to stay in Britain and those who did not.

By the 1970s, Asian immigration had slowed down. Parliament had passed laws to cut the number of people coming to Britain. However, in the 1970s, two events happened that meant that more Asians came to Britain and helped to make the Asian community one of the largest and most important in Britain.

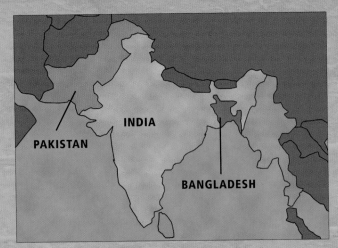

▲ A map showing the partitioning of Pakistan in 1971.

CIVIL WAR

In 1947, India and Pakistan became independent from Britain. Pakistan was split in two regions which were divided by India. These were West and East Pakistan. In 1971, East Pakistan tried to become independent of West Pakistan. After the war that followed, East Pakistan became Bangladesh. The war caused many people from Bangladesh to leave and come to Britain in search of work and stability. Most of them came from a region of Bangladesh called Sylhet. They settled in Whitechapel in East London and many of them worked in the clothing trade.

> 66 *In Brick Lane, Bengali staples such as jack fruit, betel nut and paan leaves and frozen fish caught in Sylhet's Surma river are for sale. Dozens of travel agents offer flights to Sylhet. There's a shop called Sylhet Stores. Almost everything, it seems, harks back to Sylhet.* 99
>
> The Guardian, 7 April 2005

► Mothers collecting children from primary school Whitechapel. East London. This area of London is home to many British Asians.

Some members of Britain's Muslim community have reacted angrily to what they see as attacks on their religion. In 1989 there were demonstrations against a book called *The Satanic Verses* and in 2006 some Muslims protested against cartoons of the prophet Mohammed.

FORCED FROM HOME

In the 19th and early 20th centuries, many Asians had migrated to Africa. By the end of the 1960s, some African rulers wanted to expel the Asian populations of their countries. In the late 1960s and early 1970s, Asians from Kenya began to arrive in Britain. In 1972, over 28,000 Asians who lived in Uganda were expelled. Because they had British passports many of them came to Britain and settled in the Midlands and the suburbs of North London.

▼ Asian dishes including curry have become British favourites.

SINCE THE 1970S

The Asian community in Britain has had a huge impact on the British way of life. Many of the small shops on Britain's streets are run by Asian families and Indian food is now enjoyed by just about everybody in Britain. Many cities also have large mosques and Hindu temples where Asian people worship. The Muslim festival of Eid is celebrated in London's Trafalgar Square, and the Mela Festival in Leicester is a chance for British Hindus to celebrate their faith.

▲ An Asian family expelled from Uganda in 1972. They arrived at Stradishall RAF camp at Suffolk, England.

THEN AND NOW

The first mosque was opened in Britain over 80 years ago. Today there are over 1,000 mosques.

1971
Civil war between East and West Pakistan leads to the creation of Bangladesh and the arrival of Bangladeshi immigrants.

1972
Asians are expelled from Uganda. British passport holders come to the UK.

1989
The book *The Satanic Verses* leads to protests by British Muslims.

1990
Hanif Kureishi wins the Whitbread Award for best first novel with the book *My Beautiful Laundrette*.

2001
Disturbances on the streets of cities with Asian populations, mostly in Burnley, Oldham and Bradford. London Bus and tube bombings by British Asians follow in 2005.

AFRICAN IMMIGRATION

During the 19th century large parts of Africa, particularly along the western and eastern coasts, became part of the British Empire. At the end of World War II, independence for African countries was gained very quickly. Many of these new countries went through a period of turmoil and civil war. For instance, Nigeria suffered a civil war between 1967 and 1970.

▲ A Somali family in the Hartesheik refugee camp, Eastern Ethiopia.

LOOKING FOR A BETTER LIFE

After World War II, immigration from Africa started at around the same time as countries in Africa left the British Empire and became independent. People from the West African countries of Nigeria and Ghana came to Britain in the 1960s, either to earn money to send home or to escape political unrest. Many of these Africans had lots of qualifications, but discrimination meant that many had to accept low-paid jobs.

► The Labour MP Paul Boateng is of mixed Ghanaian and Scottish heritage.

> *I have been in London three years. Now I live in Kentish Town, I live with my two brothers. I'm youngest of all my family. When I came to London I couldn't speak English. I got confused but I started college. The first time I felt shy but after a few days I was ok and all my classmates and my teacher were nice people.*

Pakawathedevy Ramanathan came to England from Somalia when she was 16 years old.

Although many Somalis came to Britain in the 1990s there has been a Somali community in Britain since World War I, and they fought in both world wars. After World War II many stayed in the port cities of Cardiff, Liverpool and London.

ESCAPING CIVIL WAR

In the 1970s and the 1990s, people from East Africa came to live in Britain. Most of them were escaping civil war and persecution in their own country. Ethiopia has had two civil wars (one in 1974 and one in 1991) and this led to thousands of Ethiopians coming to Britain. Between 1991 and 1993, troubles in Somalia also meant that men and women arrived in Britain in search of a new and safer life.

BUILDING COMMUNITIES

Most British Africans live in London. For example, it is estimated that there about 20,000 Ethiopians living in Britain but only 2,000 live outside the capital. Most Nigerians live in the London areas of Peckham, Dalston and Hackney. Ghanaians live around Dalston and Lewisham. Many Somalis live in Tower Hamlets.

▶ Many Africans have brought their own church celebrations with them. These worshippers are from the Celestial Church of Christ in South London are celebrating Harvest Festival.

BUZZ BOX

There are many famous British people who can trace their families back to Africa. The father of the MP Paul Boateng was a Ghanaian politician. The television journalist Ragi Omar and the supermodel Iman both have Somalian origins.

TIMELINE

1945-1950s
African sailors fight in World War II and then settle in the port cities of Britain.

1957
Ghana becomes independent from Britain.

1960
Nigeria becomes independent.

1963
Kenya becomes independent.

1967-70
Conflict inside Nigeria leads to many Nigerians coming to Britain.

1974
People start coming to Britain from Ethiopia, fleeing the civil war.

1991
New civil war in Ethiopia creates more immigration to Britain.

1991-1993
Civil war in Somalia encourages many people to come to Britain.

CHINESE AND VIETNAMESE IMMIGRATION

There have been Chinese people living in Britain for more than 100 years. In Victorian times a part of east London called Limehouse was Britain's first Chinatown. Now many cities have their own "Chinatown". Many of the Chinese people who came to Britain came from Hong Kong, which was controlled by Britain from 1843 to 1997, when it became part of China.

BUZZ BOX

The main part of Chinatown in Soho is Gerrard Street. Many of the buildings on this street have been built to look Chinese. It is also the centre for many Chinese festivals like New Year celebrations.

EATING OUT

During World War II, British soldiers and sailors who were sent to Hong Kong and India developed a taste for Asian food. When they returned to Britain after the war ended, they wanted to carry on eating Chinese food. This created a demand for Chinese restaurants, which encouraged more people to move to Britain from China in the 1960s.

SEARCHING FOR WORK

In the early 1960s, unemployment in a rural part of Hong Kong known as the New Territories began to rise. Many of them saw an opportunity to join in the rising demand for Chinese food in Britain and came to work in Chinese restaurants. At first it was Chinese men who came, but soon Chinese women and children came too. Most settled in Soho and Bayswater, two areas of central London. Soho is now home to Britain's largest Chinatown.

Young Chinese people who were born in Britain began to leave the restaurant trade and started many other businesses. As Chinese people became wealthier they moved to many other parts of Britain.

▲ A man stands outside Ching's Restaurant to take a photograph of London's Chinatown, 1955.

▶ A "dragon" performing a traditional dance on Chinese New Year celebrations in Chinatown, London.

▲ A group of Vietnamese "boat people" arrive in London in 1983.

THE "BOAT PEOPLE"

People from Vietnam first came to Britain in 1975 as refugees when the war between north and south Vietnam came to an end. In the late 1970s and early 1980s, many Vietnamese people tried to escape Vietnam by sailing to Hong Kong. They were known as "boat people". About 22,000 were allowed to come to Britain. At first the British government deliberately scattered these people all over the country. This did not work well, however, and Vietnamese people began to live together in cities such as London and Manchester.

> 66 *Deep in the mean streets of Liverpool's urban crisis an orchestra is rehearsing the ageless, authentic sounds of traditional Chinese music. Their tutor is Mr Li Kui Hsiung, a 43-year-old musician who has been specially imported from the People's Republic via Hong Kong to coach Europe's first traditional Chinese orchestra.* 99
>
> The Guardian, 22 October 1982

THEN AND NOW

In 1946, it was estimated that there were about 5,000 Chinese people living in Britain. In 2001 about 248,000 people in Britain described themselves as Chinese. This is less than 0.5 per cent of the British population.

TIMELINE

1945
"Chinatown" in Limehouse begins to decline and Chinese people move away.

late 1950s
Chinese restaurants start opening in Soho and Bayswater in London.

early 1960s
Chinese immigrants start to arrive from Hong Kong.

1975
End of war in Vietnam sees the first group of immigrants from Vietnam.

late 1970s-early 1980s
Vietnamese "boat people" settle all over the world, including Britain.

GREEK AND TURKISH CYPRIOT
IMMIGRATION

There are many people living in Britain who come from Greek or Turkish families. However, very few of these families actually came from Greece or Turkey. Most of them came from a small island in the Mediterranean called Cyprus, which was once part of the British Empire.

UN buffer zone
Turkish Cyprus
Greek Cyprus
UK Sovereign base areas

A DIVIDED ISLAND

The island of Cyprus is divided into Christian Greek-speaking and Muslim Turkish-speaking people. After World War II there was a lot of tension between these two groups. In the 1950s, Turkish-speaking people came to Britain to escape poverty at home. When Cyprus became independent in 1960, tension worsened and the two groups started to fight each other. This caused more people from both the Greek and Turkish sides to come to Britain.

▶ A Greek Orthodox Church in Haringey, North London.

INVASION

In 1974, the Turkish army invaded Cyprus to protect the Turkish-speaking population. The island was divided into a Greek-speaking south and a Turkish-speaking north. The Turkish part became a separate country. The Turkish-speaking people in the south of Cyprus and the Greek-speaking people in the north found themselves on the wrong side of the divide. Many of them fled to Britain to start a new life.

BUZZ BOX

Greek and Turkish-speaking Cypriots in London have their own radio stations. They play music and broadcast news about life in Cyprus, Greece and Turkey. They also have their own newspapers.

▲ Cars line Green Lanes in Haringey, North London.

TIMELINE

late 1950s
Tensions between the two groups in Cyprus sparks off Turkish Cypriot immigration to Britain.

1960
Cyprus becomes independent, sparking more Turkish-Cypriot immigration to Britain.

1974
The Cypriot government is overthrown by the army. Four days later the Turkish army invades north Cyprus. A divided Cyprus causes many more people from both sides to seek a new life in Britain.

SETTLING DOWN

Most Greek and Turkish Cypriots settled in a part of North London called Haringey. There is one particular street in Haringey called Green Lanes that is dominated by Cypriots. The Greek and Turkish-speaking Cypriots live and work next to each other along Green Lanes. On this street there are shops and community centres that serve both groups. The division in Cyprus is not seen in Britain, especially among the BBCs (British-Born Cypriots), and Greek and Turkish Cypriots work together happily.

> "*I left Cyprus because I got so fed up outside doing farming. I was a shepherd you know. At that time friends were taken on as a military police by the British Army to help them along in troublesome Cyprus. And then my dad said to me 'No, don't go there, don't go to army.' He sold the lambs, he gave me the fare and said 'Go to London to your brothers.' And I accepted that and I came over.*"
>
> Hulusi Mahmud Gurcayoglu, a Turkish Cypriot who arrived in Britain in 1958

THEN AND NOW

Cypriot immigration in the 1960s was mostly single men who came to find work. After the invasion of 1974 most of the people who came to Britain were entire families seeking safety from the conflict in Cyprus.

ITALIAN IMMIGRATION

Italians have been living in Britain for centuries. It was only during the 19th century, however, that larger numbers of Italians came to Britain to escape poverty at home. They settled in parts of London such as Clerkenwell and Soho, as well as other parts of Britain such as Scotland. After World War II the number of Italians in Britain began to increase.

LABOUR SHORTAGES

At the end of World War II, Britain found that it did not have enough workers. As well as people from the Caribbean and Asia, Italians were also encouraged to come to Britain to start a new life. Some of these Italians were prisoners of war captured by the British and were allowed to stay. However, the British government also looked for workers in a part of southern Italy called the "Mezzogiorno". This part of Italy suffered with a great deal of poverty after World War II, and many thousands took the opportunity to start a new life in Britain.

BRINGING ITALY TO BRITAIN

Although many Italians came to Britain to work in factories and other industries, some decided to start their own businesses. British-Italians (or "Britalians") have always worked in the food business and they set up restaurants and coffee bars. These sold Italian-style food and introduced a little bit of Italy to British people. Although Italians live all over Britain, London is their main home.

A SECURE AND INTERESTING JOB

London Transport wants men and women as conductors, and men of 24 or older with experience of heavy goods vehicles as drivers

SICK PAY SCHEME
PENSION SCHEME FOR MEN
FREE UNIFORM   FREE TRAVEL
GOOD CANTEENS   SPORTS CLUBS

▲ A poster from the 1950s, attempting to recruit workers from Italy.

BUZZ BOX

Scotland has produced many famous people whose families came from Italy. These include the footballer Lou Macari, the comedian Armando Iannucci, the actress Daniela Nardini and the lead singer with the band Texas, Sharleen Spiteri.

◀ Italian food has become very popular in Britain – especially pizza and pasta.

TIMELINE

1939–1945
At the start of the World War II, all Italians in Britain are arrested by the British government as Italy had sided with Germany. Italian prisoners of war are also brought to Britain.

1951
Recruitment for Italian workers begins to fill a labour shortage.

1950s–early 1960s
Italian restaurants and coffee bars open in London, and then spread throughout the rest of Britain.

MOVING TO BEDFORD

At the end of World War II there was a boom in house building. This led to more demand for bricks. One of the main centres of brick-making was in Bedford. In 1951, the brick-making companies began to recruit Italian workers for their factories. Between that date and the early 1960s nearly 7,500 Italians moved to Bedford. There are now over 14,000 "Britalians" living in Bedford. It is the largest single Italian community in Britain.

◀ An Italian brickworker in Bedford in the 1950s.

> ❝ *In the side streets, tiny greengrocers with names like La Bottega Italiani, Milita & Ciampa, and Ferretti's practically spill great bags of pasta and jugs of Chianti on the pavement, and not to speak Italian there is to be an ignorant 'foreigner'.* ❞
>
> From an article called 'Napoli, Bedfordshire' in *New Society*, April 1964

THEN AND NOW

At the start of World War II, there were about 2,000 Italians living in Britain. Today it is estimated that there are about 100,000 Italians living in Britain.

EASTERN EUROPEAN IMMIGRATION

In the 1931 British census, there were 44,462 people living in the UK who were born in Poland. This number was swelled by Poles fleeing to Britain during World War II. Until recent times these people made up the core of the present-day Polish community. By 1971, the figure had dropped to 110,925 but when Poland joined the EU in May 2004, this all changed. Over half a million Poles have since travelled to Britain in search of a new life.

STAYING AFTER THE WAR

At the start of World War II Poland was invaded by Germany and the Soviet Union. The Polish government and many Polish soldiers fled the invasion and in 1940 arrived in Britain. During the rest of the war over 20,000 Polish soldiers, sailors and airmen fought with the British against the Nazis. Most of them wanted to free Poland and return home. However, at the end of the war Poland was controlled by the Soviet Union and most Poles chose to stay in Britain.

▲ Members of the Polish army shown in 1949, having chosen to settle in Britain rather than return home. This temporary housing is actually barracks in Scotland.

BUZZ BOX

Many small towns in Britain now have large Eastern European communities. For example, the town of Crewe has become 10 per cent Polish in just three years. The tiny Scilly Isles has a population of just 2,000, but by 2005 Poles made up five per cent of its population.

BEING RESETTLED

In 1946, the British government created the Polish Resettlement Corps, which helped Polish people settle in Britain. As well as the soldiers, 33,000 dependants (wives and other relatives) came to Britain as well. At first they were housed in old army barracks but they soon moved on. Most of them moved to Earl's Court and Ealing in London.

▲ Polish migrants have filled many jobs in Britain since their country joined the European Union in 2004.

NEW EUROPEAN WORKERS

In 2004 several Eastern European countries including Estonia, Lithuania, Latvia, the Czech Republic and Poland joined the European Union. This meant that people in these countries were allowed to come to Britain to work. Since that date over half a million people have come to Britain to work mostly in building, agriculture and the hotel trade. They have settled all over the country and special shops and clubs have been set up for them. Many of them came because wages are very low in their own countries and they can earn much more in Britain.

> 66 *I've got no idea how long I am going to stay. But I'm earning so much more I now know why so many people are doing it. My sister came first and suggested that I follow. I'm living pretty cheaply with her at the moment. The papers back home are talking about how so many people have come to England to work. But people also want to live a little – that's what I am here to do.* 99
>
> David Pawlak, a 26-year-old from near Warsaw, 2006

THEN AND NOW

In the 1950s, Polish workers were involved in hard physical work like building. Many of the new Polish workers are still working in these trades but have also become important workers in agriculture and in hotels.

◄ Polish girls perform a traditional dance in London.

TIMELINE

1939
Poland is invaded by Germany and the Soviet Union.

1940
The exiled Polish government and Polish troops arrive in Britain.

1945
Poland is controlled by the Soviet Union and many Poles decide to stay in Britain.

1946
The Polish Resettlement Corps is created to help Polish people settle in Britain.

1950s
Polish people leave the army barracks they are living in and move to London.

2004
Eastern European countries (Cyprus, Czech Republic, Estonia, Hungary, Latvia, Lithuania, Malta, Poland, the Slovak Republic and Slovenia) join the European Union.

MULTICULTURAL BRITAIN

In 2001, there was a census of all the people of Britain. Everybody was asked questions about things such as their age, jobs and homes. The results of the census help to create a picture of modern Britain. One of the things that it revealed was just how multicultural Britain has become since World War II.

BUZZ BOX

One of Britain's favourite dishes is Chicken tikka masala. This is chicken cooked in a spicy gravy. Most people see it as an Asian dish. However, it was created in Britain to satisfy a British need to have gravy with their meals. This makes it a truly Asian and British meal.

WHAT THE CENSUS SHOWS

Although the census revealed that seven out of eight people in Britain described themselves as "White British", this still meant that about 13 per cent of people living in Britain described themselves in another way. There are now over two million people who see themselves as Asian. Over 25 per cent of people in Leicester are Indian and Tower Hamlets in London is over 33 per cent Bangladeshi. Parts of London are now over 10 ten per cent Caribbean or African.

DIFFERENT FAITHS

The census also asked people about their religious beliefs. The answers that people gave showed another picture of multicultural Britain. The largest religious group are Christians. The second most common religion in Britain is Islam. Just over three per cent of Britain's population is Muslim. Hindus make up about 1.5 per cent of Britain and less than 0.5 per cent of British people are Jewish.

▼ This class from a school in South London shows the multicultural make-up of today's Britain.

> *"When people ask me where I am from I say I am British, even though I am of Chinese origin. I am proud to say I am British and have always thought of myself as such. I am proud to come from a country which welcomed my parents and which has given me the freedom to do what I want without being discriminated against because of my sex or race."*

Michelle Wong, a British-Chinese woman talking about her experiences in Britain

1997
Mohammed Sarwar becomes Britain's first Muslim MP.

2002
Paul Boateng becomes Britain's first black government Minister.

2004
Britain's first black Chief Constable, Mike Fuller, is appointed to lead the Kent force.

2005
The soldier Johnson Beharry becomes the first black British soldier to win the Victoria Cross.

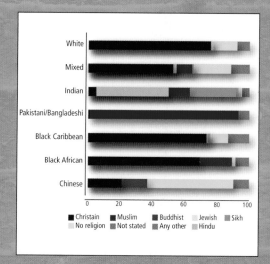

▲ A chart showing the percentage of Britons belonging to various religions.

LIVING IN MULTICULTURAL BRITAIN

From the music that we enjoy hearing to the food that we eat, the arrival of different groups in Britain has had a huge impact on the way that all of us live our lives. Britain has also changed the way that immigrants have lived their lives. Events such as the Mela (a Hindu festival) or Eid (a Muslim festival) are now celebrated in many parts of Britain and all people are welcome to join in. Immigration has changed Britain and all of us, no matter where we come from, are part of that change.

THEN AND NOW

It was in 1991 when people were first asked about their ethnic origins. Between that date and 2001, the number of people in Britain who described themselves as Caribbean, Asian, African or Chinese rose from six per cent to 9 per cent. The proportion of Chinese people rose from 0.3 per cent in 1991 to 0.4 per cent in 2001.

> *"We celebrate the diversity in our country; get strength from the cultures and the races that go to make up Britain today."*

The former prime minister Tony Blair speaking in 2005

▶ The popular band The Sugababes reflect the cosmopolitan make-up and influences of Britain.

GLOSSARY

Asian	Term used to describe people from East, Southeast and South Asia
Boat people	A phrase used to describe the Vietnamese people who settled in Britain in the late 1970s and early 1980s
British Empire	Parts of the world that were controlled by the British. The empire was at its largest at the end of the 19th century. Most of the countries controlled by Britain are now independent
Caribbean	A large group of islands close to the United States of America. The most important islands are Jamaica, Bermuda and Barbados
Chinatown	An area of a large city with a large Chinese population and a wide variety of Chinese restaurants and shops. The largest Chinatown is in London
Civil war	A conflict between two or more groups of people inside the same country
Commonwealth	A voluntary association of independent nations and dependent territories linked by historical ties (as parts of the former British Empire) and working together on matters of shared interest
Discrimination	When somebody is treated unfairly for reasons such as skin colour or religion
Immigrant	A person who leaves one country to go and live in another country
Independent	Countries that rule themselves
Multi-cultural	A word to describe a country with many different groups of people living together
Muslim	One of the largest religious groups in Britain. Most British Muslim families originally came from Pakistan or Bangladesh
Racism	When somebody is treated unfairly because of the colour of their skin or because of their ethnic origins
Riots	When a group of people fight with symbols of authority such as the police
West Indies	Another name for the islands of the Caribbean

Websites

www.movinghere.org.uk/
A website that explores the experiences of Caribbean, Irish, Jewish and Asian immigrants to Britain over the past 200 years

www.blackpresence.co.uk/
A website that looks at the impact of Caribbean and African communities on modern Britain

www.bbc.co.uk/history/british/modern/windrush_01.shtml
A BBC website that looks at the arrival of the Empire Windrush and its impact on Britain

http://www.theasiannews.co.uk/
News relating to Asian communities in Britain

www.asht.info/
The Anglo-Sikh Heritage Trail website looks at the impact of the Sikh community on modern Britain

www.plantcultures.org.uk/
Explores the link between Britain and Asia through plants and people

www.empiremuseum.co.uk/index.htm
The British Empire and Commonwealth Museum website has a lot of information on immigration to Britain

Note to parents and teachers: Every effort has been made by the Publishers to ensure that these websites are suitable for children, that they are of the highest educational value, and that they contain no inappropriate or offensive material. However, because of the nature of the Internet, it is impossible to guarantee that the contents of these sites will not be altered. We strongly advise that Internet access is supervised by a responsible adult.

INDEX